Dry Bones Presents:
Jewish Curses
a Guide and Coloring Book
by
Yaakov Kirschen

Part of the
"Grandpa's Jewish Cartoon Coloring Books"
Series

A special thanks to Sali Ariel,
the LSW (Long Suffering Wife)
for her work in selecting cartoons,
editing, and helping to
make this book a reality.

ABOUT THE "GRANDPA'S JEWISH CARTOON COLORING BOOKS" SERIES

The European Jewish immigrants who came to our English-speaking world brought with them a secret language called Yiddish. It was a cultural treasure, a language which only they could speak. It was a tool to express their unique and special world view.

Cartoonist Yaakov Kirschen is an old guy. Mr. Shuldig, the bald hero of his Dry Bones cartoons is also an old guy. Now, after more than four decades of writing and drawing his daily Israeli/American political cartoon, Kirschen has decided to tackle something REALLY important; passing on the essence of Yiddish culture to a younger generation and warming the hearts of other old guys and gals.

Yiddish so strongly carried within it the unique essence of European Jewish culture that after Yiddish disappeared from common usage, much of it still manages to survive in English. It is the purpose of the "Grandpa's Jewish Cartoon Coloring Books" series to assist in the transmission of the special flavor of Yiddish and Yiddishisms to new generations of Jews and to ignite the warm memories of older generations.

We hope that you will enjoy reading these pages and have the fun of coloring the cartoons.

JEWISH CURSES AND JEWISH CURSING.

This book is not about cursing as in the kind of "cursing" you do when you hit your thumb with a hammer.

This book focuses on a uniquely Jewish art form which combines anger and aggressive humor in a blend that is at its core, funny. In its purest structure the Jewish curse is father to the Jewish joke one-liner. The curses in this book are all translations from the original Yiddish and no effort has been made to make them more understandable or funny in English. I hope that, with a little effort, you will find them a door to understanding the mindset, attitudes, and native wit of our Yiddish immigrant past, a native wit that was rich in what we now call Jewish humor.

Most of these curses are in two parts; the first part is usually an upbeat blessing as in *"May you win the lottery. . ."* which is then followed by a zinger like *"and spend it all on doctors"*.

Others are incredibly creative in their surrealistic nastiness; "May *all your teeth fall out except one. And in that one you should have a tooth ache!"* Note that the two part structure is maintained except that the first part is nasty rather than upbeat, and the second part tops it in nastiness!

With these concepts in place, let us begin,

with love,

Kirschen.

Yaakov Kirschen
DryBones.com

Instructions

1. Turn off your phone, shut down your computer, and prepare yourself for some quiet private time.

2. Pick the cartoon page you'd like to color. Some are intense and complicated, others are simple to color, Decide on the experience you are looking for.

3. You can color with colored pencils, gel pens, markers, or crayons. To test how they'll look on the pages of this coloring book. Use the "Test Your Colors" page.

4. Be sure to slip a piece of paper behind the test page to protect the page behind it from possible bleed through.

5. After selecting your colors, turn to the page you are going to color (remember to slip a piece of paper behind the page you plan to color to protect the next page from possible bleed through).

6. Note that all pages to color are printed on one side only for better results. After coloring a cartoon you might want to cut out the page and frame your work.

7. It's now time to free your mind from the annoying pressures that haunt you. It's time to lose yourself in coloring and Jewish curses. Good Luck. Happy Coloring. You deserve a laugh and a little healthy relaxation.

Test Your Colors Page

Test your pencil, pen, brush or crayon's effect on the paper and ink used in this coloring book by filling in one or part of one of the circles. Slide a piece of paper behind this page to protect against "bleed through".

The Curses

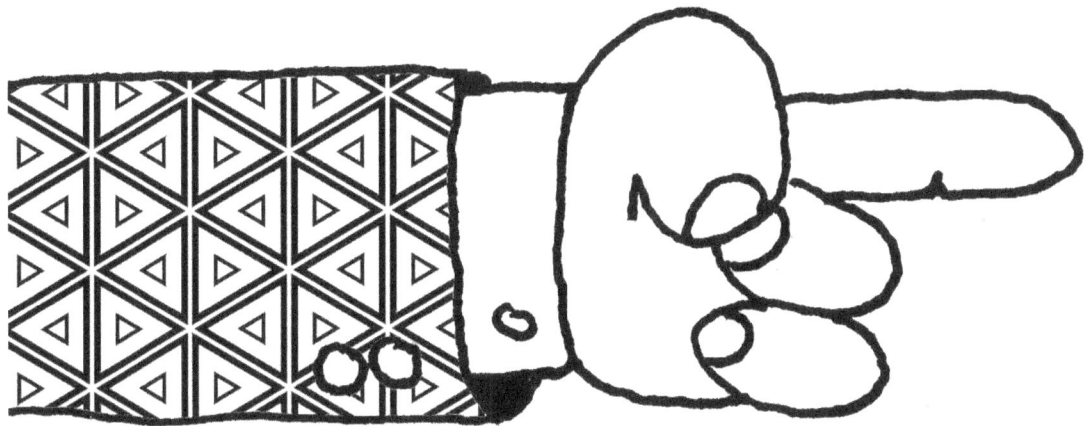

May you win the lottery
and spend it all on doctors.

May you have a large store, and whatever people ask for, you shouldn't have . . . and what you do have, No one should want.

May you find a gold piece on the sidewalk and be so arthritic you can't pick it up.

May you become so rich that every day your chauffer should drive you in your expensive limousine to a different specialist and nobody should know what's wrong with you!

May you live in a house with a hundred rooms, and may each room have its own bed, and may you wander every night from room to room, and from bed to bed, unable to sleep.

May you grow so rich that your widow's second husband never has to worry about making a living.

May your daughter's beauty be admired by everyone else in the circus sideshow.

May you forever be alone with the person you love the most, you yourself

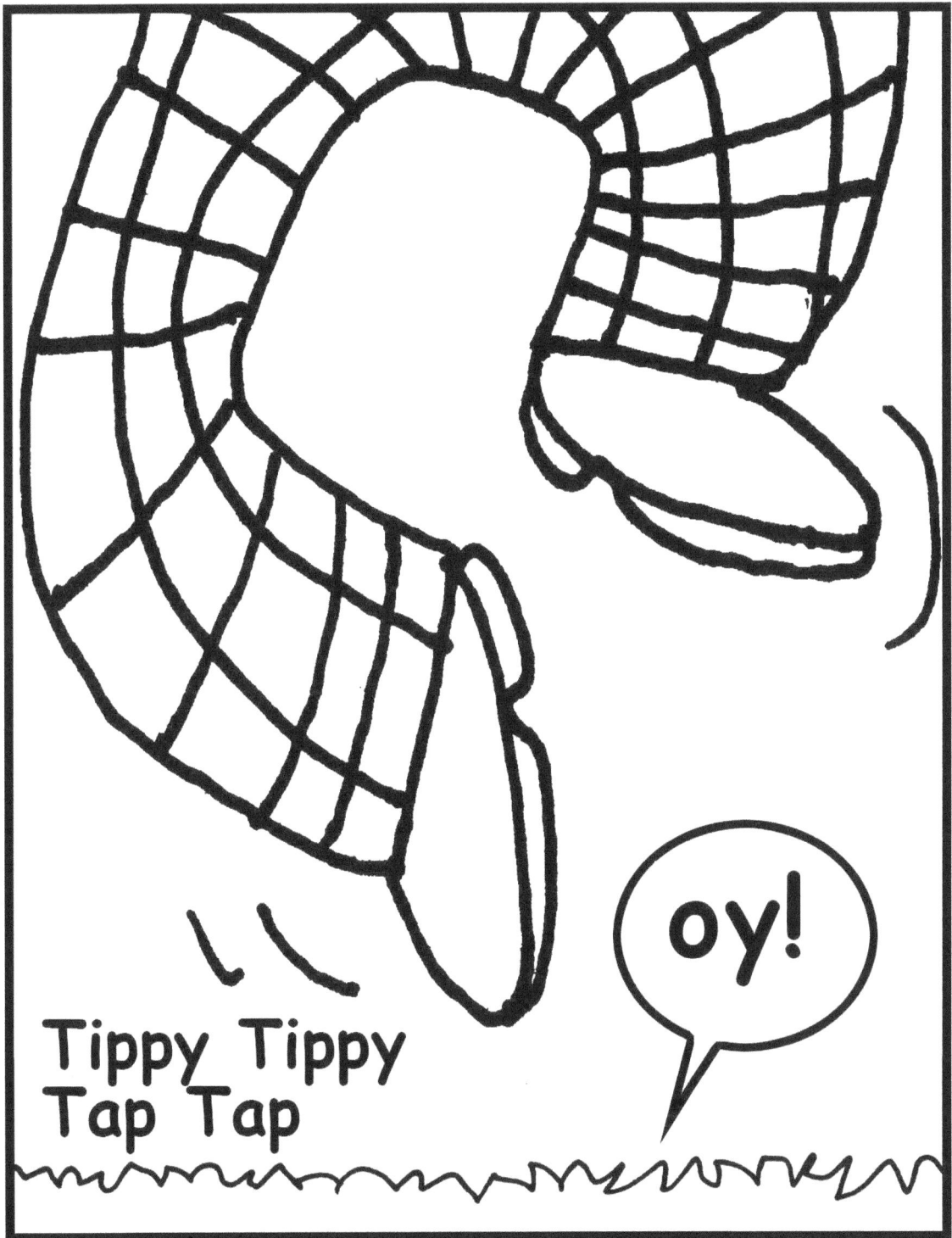

May your enemies sprain their ankles dancing on your grave.

May you have a sweet death;
a truck full of sugar should run
over you!

May your daughter's hair grow thick and abundant, all over her face!

They should call a doctor for you urgently and when he arrives they should tell him that they don't need him anymore!

May you lose all your teeth except one ...and in that one tooth you should have a tooth ache.

May your bones be broken as often as the Ten Commandments.

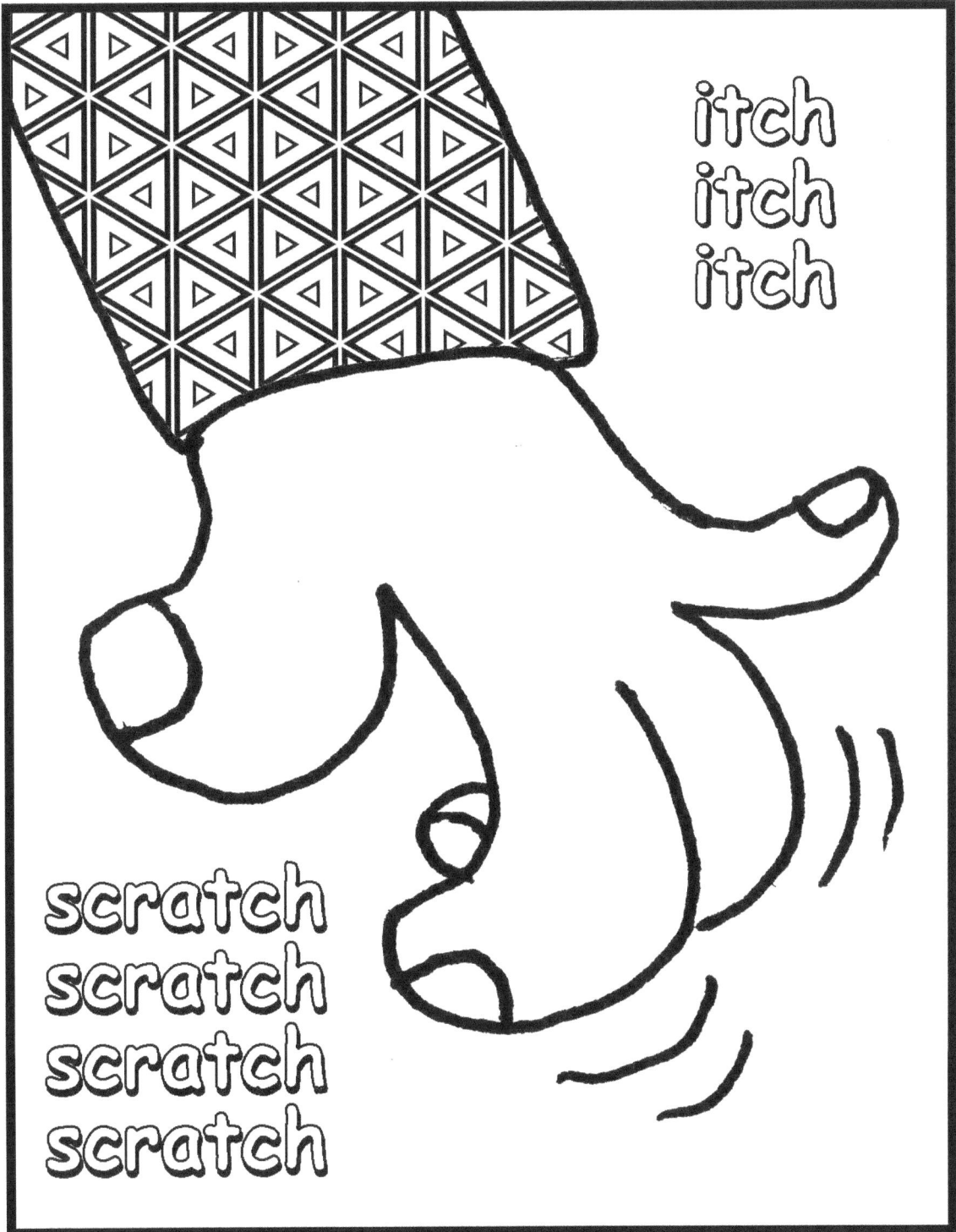

May the lice in your shirt marry the bedbugs in your mattress and may their offspring set up residence in your underwear.

May you need an operation that only one doctor in the world is able to perform, and may that doctor refuse because you can't pay his fee, and may that doctor be your only son.

May you have a good long sleep ... and may all your dreams be only about your troubles.

May you live until 120 . . .
with a wooden head and a glass eye.

May you be known for your tolerance and for being the proof that people can endure any kind of hardship.

May you struggle to stay awake during the day, and find it impossible to fall asleep during the night.

May you always have one nostril clogged.

May your wife eat matzohs in bed and may you roll in the crumbs.

May your mother-in-law treat you like her very own daughter ...and move in with you!

May your head be full of lice
but your arms too short for you
to scratch.

May the sun and the spring breeze warm you and caress you like an apple . . . as you hang from a tree.

May onions grow in your bellybutton.

May you love good food so much that you turn into a blintz, and may your enemy turn into a cat, and may he catch you, eat you up, and choke on you . . . So we can be rid of the two of you.

May they let a madman out of his cell . . . and put you into it instead.

May you smell so bad that goats, skunks, and pigs will refuse to ride in the same wagon with you.

DON'T BE A STRANGER

After you've enjoyed this book, please be on the lookout for more volumes in the "Grandpa's Jewish Cartoon Coloring Books" series.

Yaakov Kirschen (Dry Bones)
and Mr. Shuldig
www.drybones.com

www.ingramcontent.com/pod-product-compliance
Lightning Source LLC
Chambersburg PA
CBHW081522040426
42447CB00013B/3310